THE OLYMPICS
HISTORY

THE OLYMPICS
HISTORY

Moira Butterfield

W

FRANKLIN WATTS
LONDON • SYDNEY

First published in 2011 by Franklin Watts

Franklin Watts
338 Euston Road
London NW1 3BH

Franklin Watts Australia
Level 17/207 Kent Street
Sydney, NSW 2000

A CIP catalogue record for this book
is available from the British Library.

Dewey no: 796.4'8'09

ISBN: 978 1 4451 0270 2

Printed in China.

Franklin Watts is a division of Hachette Children's Books, an Hachette UK company

www.hachette.co.uk

Series editor: Sarah Ridley
Editor in chief: John C. Miles
Designer: Jason Billin
Art director: Jonathan Hair
Picture research: Diana Morris

Picture credits: Ace Stock/Alamy: 6bl. Arup/Rex Features: 27. BCMF Arquitectos: 29. Bettmann/Corbis: 17b, 18br. Adrian Dennis/AFP/Getty Images: 28c. Mary Evans PL: 9. Getty Images: 8b, 11t, 12. John Gichigi/Getty Images: 26. The Granger Collection/Topfoto: 13bl, 17t, 18bl. Hulton Archive/Getty Images: 10. Hulton-Deutsch/Corbis: front cover. Impact/Alamy: 6b. Jacques Langevin/Sygma/Corbis: 24. Library of Congress: 8t. LOCOG: 28b. mary416/Shutterstock: 25. Wally McNamee/Corbis: 23t. Gianni d'agli Orti/Museo Nazionale Terme, Roma/Art Archive: 7. Picturepoint/Topham: 14t, 14b, 15. Mike Powell/Getty Images: 22. Gerard Ranciman, Jean Guichard/Sygma/Corbis: 20. Jean-Yves Ruszniewski/TempSport/Corbis: 5, 23b. Sports Illustrated/Getty Images: 21t, 21b. Topfoto: 3, 11b, 19. ullsteinbild/Topfoto: 13r. World History Archive/Topfoto: 16.

Every attempt has been made to clear copyright. Should there be any inadvertent omission please apply to the publisher for rectification.

Note to parents and teachers

Every effort has been made by the Publishers to ensure that the websites in this book are suitable for children, that they are of the highest educational value, and that they contain no inappropriate or offensive material. However, because of the nature of the Internet, it is impossible to guarantee that the contents of these sites will not be altered. We strongly advise that Internet access is supervised by a responsible adult.

CONTENTS

Downloadable activity and information sheets
are available at www.franklinwatts.co.uk

THE BIRTH OF THE OLYMPICS

The first recorded Olympic Games took place in 776 BCE, at Olympia in ancient Greece. Like the modern Olympics, they were held every four years. They continued for 1,100 years until 393 CE.

The ancient Greeks believed that competitive sport pleased their gods, so they held the Games on a sacred temple site. At the Opening Ceremony they lit a flame at the altar of Zeus, King of the Gods, and kept it burning until the Games ended. In the earliest Olympics there was only one event – the 'stadion', a sprint of almost 200 metres. A crowd up to 40,000-strong watched from the stadium.

◀ An ancient Greek vase showing Olympic wrestlers.

▼ The remains of the running track at Olympia, including stone starting blocks for the athletes.

Amazing Olympics

If a cheat was discovered at the ancient Olympics, the athlete was disqualified, whipped and had to pay a fine, which was used to make a statue of Zeus.

The athletes

Ancient Greece was divided into separate city states. Athletes represented their own city state, called a 'polis'. Eventually competitors came from other parts of Europe and North Africa, too. The winners won a laurel wreath and a palm frond. Back home they were treated as stars and given valuable perks, such as free food. The main Olympics were for male athletes only as women had their own separate event.

The events

Gradually there were more events, such as boxing, wrestling and a violent mixture of the two called the 'pankration'. More sprint races were added along with chariot-racing, long jump, discus and javelin throwing. As well as sport there was an artistic side to the Games. Sculptors and poets carved statues of the star athletes or wrote poetry about them.

▶ An ancient statue showing an Olympic discus thrower. All athletes competed naked at the Games.

Olympic facts and stats

First recorded champion Koroibos, a Greek cook, was the first recorded winner of the stadion race.

Most successful champion The runner Leonidas of Rhodes, who won 12 times between 164 BCE and 152 BCE.

Most famous celebrity Wrestler Milon of Kroton (in southern Italy), who won six times between 540 BCE and 516 BCE. He was a great showman who once carried a bull into the Olympic arena.

First female champion Kyniska of Sparta was declared winner of chariot races in 396 BCE and 392 BCE, even though she was the team-owner and trainer and didn't actually take part.

7

OLYMPICS REBORN

The Olympics were revived in 1896 through the efforts of Frenchman Baron Pierre de Coubertin.

At first Baron de Coubertin found it difficult to get the Games going again, but he persevered and the first modern Olympics were held in Athens, Greece, in 1896. There were 43 events, including some unusual ones such as one-handed weight-lifting and a swimming race only open to members of the Greek Navy. There were 245 competitors, all of them men, from 14 countries.

Setting up the IOC

Baron de Coubertin set up the International Olympic Committee (IOC for short), which still sets the rules and organises the Summer and Winter Olympics today. Its members come from the National Olympic Committees of the countries taking part, and between them they decide where the Olympics will be held.

△ Baron de Coubertin

▽ Crowds cheer Greek hero Spiridon Louis as he wins the marathon at Athens, Greece, in 1896.

⬥ The start of the first-ever modern Olympic race, a heat for the 100 metre event at Athens, Greece, in 1896.

Moving on

The next two Olympic Games were held in Paris, France in 1900 and St. Louis, USA in 1904. Women took part for the first time in 1900, where there were more surprising events, such as the equestrian (horse) high jump and a swimming obstacle race where competitors had to climb poles and swim under boats.

Amazing Olympics

In the first Olympic Games the winners got a silver medal and the runners-up received a bronze. In the second Olympic Games they all received trophies instead. Gold, silver and bronze medals were first awarded at the third Games.

Olympic facts and stats

1896 The first modern Olympic Games were held in Athens, Greece.

1900 The first female Olympic champion, Charlotte Cooper of Great Britain, won the women's tennis event at the Paris Olympics.

1904 The first Africans to compete in the Olympics ran in the marathon event in St. Louis, USA. They were Tswana tribesmen who happened to be taking part in an exhibition nearby.

1904 American gymnast George Eyser won three gold medals, two silvers and a bronze, despite having a wooden leg.

FASTER, HIGHER, STRONGER

From 1908 to 1928 the Olympics became more organised, and many more countries took part. The first Winter Olympics were held in Chamonix, France, in 1924.

Gradually the Olympics gained features that are still used today. In 1908 the athletes marched into the stadium for the first time, nation by nation, and in 1912 electronic timing was introduced. At the Antwerp Games in 1920 the Olympic flag was flown, with five rings representing the continents from which the athletes are drawn: Africa, America, Europe, Asia and Oceania. The white background symbolises peace.

Amazing Olympics

At the 1912 Games in Stockholm, Sweden, the longest-ever Olympic cycling race took place over 320 kilometres. The winner finished in just under 11 hours.

The Norwegian team parade behind their national flag at the 1908 Opening Ceremony in London.

Taking the oath

An athlete took the Olympic Oath for the first time in 1920, something that still happens at the beginning of every Olympic Games. One chosen competitor repeats the Oath on behalf of every athlete taking part.

The Olympic motto

The IOC introduced an Olympic motto in 1924: *Citius, Altius, Fortius*, which is Latin for 'Faster, Higher, Stronger'. It also introduced the Olympic Creed, which explains the ideals behind the Games:

"The most important thing in the Olympic Games is not to win but to take part, just as the most important thing in life is not the triumph, but the struggle. The essential thing is not to have conquered, but to have fought well."

In 1920 Belgian Victor Boin became the first athlete ever to take the Olympic Oath.

A female competitor in an early shot-put event.

Olympic facts and stats

1908 The first brother and sister medallists, Willy and Lottie Dod of Great Britain, won archery medals.

1920 The oldest ever Olympic competitor, Swede Oscar Swahn, won a silver medal in a deer-shooting competition, aged 72.

1920 The tug-of-war appeared as an event in the Olympics for the last time.

1928 Women were allowed to compete in gymnastics and track and field events for the first time.

The Second World War overshadowed the Olympics between 1932 and 1948. Despite this, sporting heroes and new innovations made the Games a better show.

In 1932, at the Los Angeles Games, the male athletes stayed in their own Olympic Village for the first time. The female athletes stayed in a luxury hotel. Living quarters were not so comfortable at the London Games in 1948 because the UK was recovering from the Second World War (1939–45). Athletes stayed in RAF camps, schools and colleges. Today Olympic venues always have a purpose-built Olympic Village.

Hitler's Games

In 1936, the Olympic Games were held in Berlin, Germany. The Nazi leader Adolf Hitler tried to use the Olympics to showcase his Nazi Party and particularly his racist views that Aryans – white-skinned Germans – were superior in every way to other peoples. The black American sprinter and long-jumper Jesse Owens proved him spectacularly wrong by winning five gold medals.

Nazi swastikas decorated the stadium at the 1936 Olympics in Berlin, Germany.

Amazing Olympics

Hollywood film stars, such as Marlene Dietrich, Gary Cooper and Charlie Chaplin, entertained the crowds at the 1932 Games in Los Angeles, USA.

Olympic facts and stats

1932 This was the first Games to take place over 16 days. Previous Olympics had been spread over four or five months.

1932 Sprinter Liu Changchun became the first Chinese competitor in the Olympics.

1936 All athletes were supposed to shout *Sieg Heil* (a Nazi slogan) and salute as they passed Adolf Hitler at the Opening Ceremony. Those who didn't were booed.

1940/1944 These Games were cancelled due to the Second World War.

1948 US sprinter Audrey Patterson became the first black woman to win an Olympic medal.

Carrying the flame

At the Berlin Games in 1936 the Olympic flame was carried by relay from Olympia in Greece to the Olympic stadium for the first time. Over the years the flame has been carried in many different ways, including boat, aeroplane, on horseback and by dog sled.

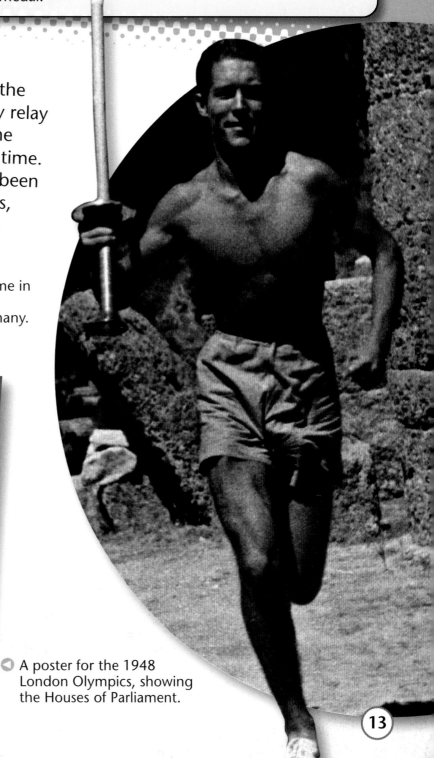

▶ An athlete carries the Olympic flame in 1936. It was taken by relay from Olympia in Greece to Berlin, Germany.

◀ A poster for the 1948 London Olympics, showing the Houses of Parliament.

COLD WAR OLYMPICS

As TV and radio coverage grew, the Olympics became more and more popular. However, during the 1950s they were affected by the Cold War – hostility and suspicion between the Communist countries of the Soviet Union and the democratic countries of Western Europe and the USA.

At the 1952 Helsinki Games the Soviet Union entered the competition for the first time. Their athletes had followed very focused training programmes and came away with many medals. Sport became a sort of fake war

Czech long-distance runner Emile Zatopek won three golds at the 1952 Olympics.

The Opening Ceremony in Melbourne, Australia, in 1956. Photography was still black and white.

between democratic and Communist countries, and sporting triumphs were seen as symbols of the success of either side. Some athletes from Communist countries defected, refusing to go home after the Games and asking for political asylum in the West.

Protestors and boycotts

The Games became the focus for protests and boycotts, because they gave protestors a chance to get worldwide publicity. Arab countries withdrew from the 1956 Summer Olympics in protest at Israeli military actions, whilst some European countries refused to take part in protest at the Soviet invasion of Hungary.

A new Closing Ceremony

In 1956, the Closing Ceremony changed. Instead of marching into the stadium country by country, all the athletes came in together, to show friendship and unity. This continues today.

▷ The water-polo final in 1956 descended into a punch-up between the Hungarian and Soviet teams, as tensions flared after the Soviet invasion of Hungary in 1956.

Amazing Olympics

Every Olympic Games has an official number and the title 'Olympiad'. For instance, the 2012 London Games will be the Thirtieth Olympiad (XXX in Roman numerals).

Olympic facts and stats

1952 Lisa Hartel of Denmark won a silver medal in a riding event despite being paralysed below the knee by polio. She was helped on and off her horse to compete.

1956 The Games in Melbourne, Australia, were the first ones held in the Southern Hemisphere.

1956 During the Melbourne Games the horse events had to be held in Stockholm, Sweden, because animal quarantine laws prevented horses entering Australia.

1956 American weight-lifter Charles Vinci was over the weight limit for his event, but managed to qualify by cutting off his hair at the very last minute to lose 200 grammes.

During the 1960s, politics continued to cause trouble at the Olympics. The Games grew in size and, in 1960, the first Paralympic Games were held a few weeks after the Summer Games.

Politics began to play a big part in the Olympic story. During the 1968 Olympics in Mexico City, two African-American sprinters staged a silent protest for black civil rights during the medal ceremony for the 200-metre sprint. They were promptly banned from the Games and from Mexico. Meanwhile South Africa was banned from the Olympics because of its racist apartheid government policy, which segregated black and white South Africans (kept them separate in schools, jobs and towns).

Drugs testing and sports science
The first drugs disqualification occurred in 1968 after a Swedish athlete tested positive for having too much alcohol in his blood. Sports science was still very under-developed compared to modern times.

US Olympic medal-winning athletes make a 'Black Power' salute in 1968, to support the fight for black civil rights in the USA.

Amazing Olympics

Sex-testing for women was introduced for the first time in the Mexico Games of 1968, to make sure that competitors were actually female.

Olympic facts and stats

1960 During the Rome Olympics some events were held on ancient Roman sites, such as the 2,000-year-old site of a wrestling ring.

1964 The Tokyo Olympics were the first to be held in Asia.

1964 The first Olympic wedding took place when two Bulgarian athletes got married in the Tokyo Olympic Village.

1964 Abebe Bikila of Ethiopia won the marathon just six weeks after having his appendix out.

For instance, nowadays athletes have a carefully worked-out scientific programme of training to help them deal with hot conditions, but in 1960 British walker Don Thompson prepared for the heat of Rome in summer by training in a bathroom full of heaters and boiling kettles.

TV and broadcasting revenue

The Olympics were shown on colour TV for the first time in the 1960s. The new technology meant that the IOC could begin to sell broadcasting rights to TV companies around the world. At first they charged a few hundred thousand pounds, but in 2012 the sale of the broadcasting rights for the London Summer Olympics is expected to earn the IOC nearly £2 billion.

JEUX DE LA XVII OLYMPIADE

ROMA 25.VIII-11.IX

ROMA MCMLX

◖ A poster for the 1960 Rome Olympics.

◗ An exhausted athlete in Mexico City, 1968. Because Mexico City is located at a high altitude, there is less oxygen in the air than normal, making running extra tough.

In the 1970s the Olympics saw tragedy, but also celebrated extraordinary performances that captivated the TV-watching world.

Tragedy and violence hit the 1972 Munich Olympics when Palestinian terrorists broke into the Olympic Village and took members of the Israeli team hostage. Eleven Israeli team-members, five terrorists and a policeman died, and the Olympics were suspended until the IOC decided to go on with the Games. Since the incident, security has become much tighter at international sports events.

Screen fame

Despite troubles off the track, the Olympic sporting triumphs of the 1970s were enjoyed by millions of people because home TVs had become much more common. Amongst the athletes who became household names were US swimmer Mark Spitz and Russian gymnast Olga Korbut. Then in 1976 Romanian gymnast Nadia Comãneci won the first-ever perfect gymnastics score of 10.00.

⚫ Gymnast Olga Korbut won four golds and two silvers in 1972 and 1976.

◀ US swimmer Mark Spitz won seven golds in Munich, Germany, in 1972.

▲ Paralympic athletes take part in a basketball game in the 1970s.

The Paralympics

Until 1976 only wheelchair competitors could take part in the Paralympics, but now the IOC changed its rules to allow other disabilities, too. In 1976 disabled skiers competed in the first Paralympic Winter Olympics in Sweden. Now thousands of disabled athletes compete in all kinds of summer and winter Olympic sports.

Amazing Olympics

The 1972 Munich Olympics had the first cartoon mascot – Waldi the dachshund dog. Now every Olympic Games has an official mascot.

Olympic facts and stats

1972 British horse Cornishman V appeared in Hollywood films as well as helping his riders to win two gold medals.

1972 A German student disguised as an athlete joined the marathon race near the end and pretended to be the winner. The real winner arrived a few minutes later.

1976 Japanese gymnast Shun Fujimoto carried on competing with a broken kneecap, gritting his teeth and not telling anyone, to help his team win gold.

1976 The Winter Games were awarded to Denver, USA, but residents voted against paying for it, so the Games had to move to Innsbruck, Austria.

TV TIMES

In the 1980s business sponsors began to invest in the Olympics, buying the right to get their products displayed and advertised during the event. The organisers of the Olympics needed the money because the cost of staging the Games now ran into billions.

Although Olympic athletes were meant to be amateur (earning no money from their sport), Communist countries supported their athletes full time, so they didn't need other jobs and had lots more time to train. This forced the IOC to change the rules in 1988 to allow most Olympic athletes to be professionals. They were allowed to get sponsorship – regular money – from businesses such as sports equipment manufacturers, and they were allowed to advertise products.

The 1984 Los Angeles Olympics was the first privately funded Olympic Games, supported by businesses and sponsorship deals.

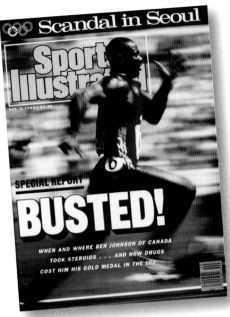

Scandal in Seoul

Sport Illustrated

SPECIAL REPORT

BUSTED!

WHEN AND WHERE BEN JOHNSON OF CANADA TOOK STEROIDS . . . AND HOW DRUGS COST HIM HIS GOLD MEDAL IN THE 100

◀ Ben Johnson hit the headlines for taking drugs. He was stripped of his gold medal.

Illegal drugs and more boycotts

Soon the IOC was dealing with a different type of problem – illegal drugs. In 1988 Ben Johnson, Olympic 100-metre sprint champion, became the most famous athlete at the time to test positive for a performance-enhancing drug and he was stripped of his medal. Added to this the Olympics were affected by politics again. Countries led by the USA pulled out of the 1980 Games in Moscow to protest against the Soviet invasion of Afghanistan, and in 1984 the Soviets organised their own boycott in revenge.

Opening Ceremony

The Opening Ceremony at the 1984 Los Angeles Olympics was a huge theatrical show. Five giant Olympic rings were lit, there were pop-star performers and a rocket man who flew into the stadium. Since then opening ceremonies have become a massive event watched by millions.

Amazing Olympics

At every Olympic Games new sports are added and old ones are dropped. At the 1984 Olympics, synchronised swimming appeared for the first time.

▶ In 1984 synchronised swimming became an Olympic sport, with team and individual events.

Olympic facts and stats

1984 McDonald's paid $4 million (£2.5 million) to have the Olympic swimming pool named after the company.

1984 Women ran the marathon for the first time. Decades before doctors had banned women from running long distances in case they 'became old too soon'.

1988 At the Calgary Winter Olympics the Jamaican bobsled team appeared for the first time, inspiring the film *Cool Runnings*.

1988 US diver Greg Louganis won gold despite hitting his head on the diving board during qualifying rounds.

NEW HOPE

In the 1990s the Cold War ended and the Soviet Union split up into 15 different countries, while East and West Germany became one nation. The list of Olympic nations and the medal-winning results tables began to look very different.

At the Barcelona Olympics in 1992 South Africa competed for the first time since 1960, after the ending of Apartheid. The new era was symbolised by the women's 10,000-metre race, which was a close-run contest between Derartu Tulu of Ethiopia and white South African athlete Elana Meyer. Tulu took gold, Meyer silver, then the two athletes ran a victory lap together to show the new mood of peace and co-operation.

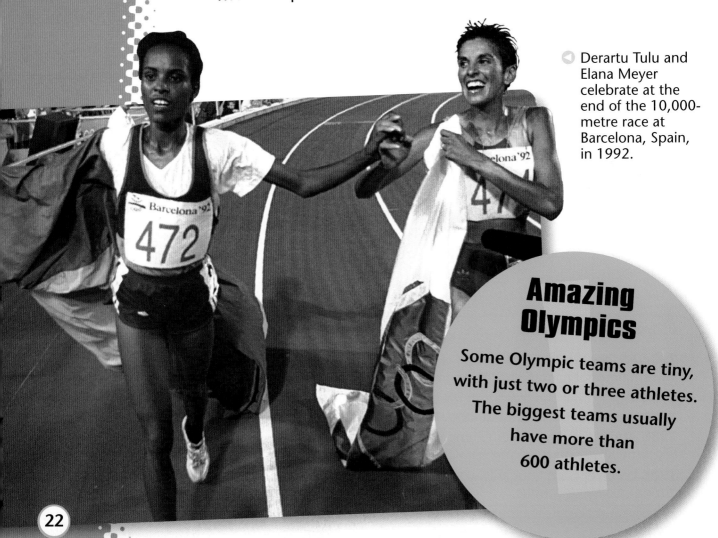

Derartu Tulu and Elana Meyer celebrate at the end of the 10,000-metre race at Barcelona, Spain, in 1992.

Amazing Olympics

Some Olympic teams are tiny, with just two or three athletes. The biggest teams usually have more than 600 athletes.

Merchandising

A logo and slogan are designed for each Olympic Games. In the 1990s these emblems began to appear on lots of merchandise, including hats, T-shirts and mugs. Companies pay for a licence – the right to use the logo on all sorts of different goods. The Atlanta Games in 1996 made a record $50 million (£32 million) from licensing, and since that time the figure has grown.

Host cities

The IOC chooses a new venue nine years before an Olympic Games is due to take place. The countries bidding for the Games make a presentation to convince the IOC to choose them. After some IOC members were found to have taken bribes in 1998, bidding rules have been tightened up.

A branded jacket worn at the 1996 Olympics. At every Games you can buy items showing the official emblems.

Ross Rebagliati, the first-ever Olympic snowboarding champion, at the Winter Olympic Games in 1998.

Olympic facts and stats

1992 At the Barcelona Olympics, Chinese diver Fu Mingxia won gold at the age of 13. Spanish rowing cox Carlos Front was the youngest competitor, aged 11.

1996 Austrian sailor Hubert Raudaschl competed in a record ninth Olympic Games.

1996 The giant Olympic stadium torch was lit in Atlanta, USA, by world-famous boxer Muhammad Ali.

1998 Snowboarding became an Olympic winter sport for the first time.

In the 2000s the Olympics grew larger, more hi-tech and more expensive, too. At the Beijing Olympics in 2008 over 11,000 athletes from 204 nations competed in 302 events. The event cost about £25 billion to stage.

In 2000 the Games went to Sydney, Australia, and in 2004 they returned to Greece, where some events were held at the ancient stadium of Olympia. The Olympic slogan for the Greek Olympics was 'Welcome Home'. In 2008 the Beijing Games drew the biggest TV audience ever, with an estimated 4.7 billion viewers and an opening ceremony that lasted four hours and had 15,000 performers. The crowds saw an athlete ignite the giant Olympic torch as he flew across the stadium.

Amazing Olympics

The Beijing Games began at 8pm on 8 August 2008, because the number 8 is considered lucky in China.

The Olympic rings on Sydney Harbour Bridge, Australia, during the 2000 Olympics.

Running the Games

The Games were now so big that hundreds of thousands of people were needed to keep all the events running smoothly. There had to be a Technology Operations Centre manned by experts to control the many thousands of computers and phone links. The organisers of the Beijing Olympics even used traditional *feng shui* to plan the position of their new stadiums, believing this would help to bring peace and harmony to the Games.

New drugs-testing

The IOC cracked down on drug-takers, using hi-tech testing methods to catch cheating athletes. They set up the World Anti-Doping Agency, which began testing Olympic athletes at thousands of sports events outside of the Olympic Games themselves. Competitors who tested positive were banned and had their medals taken away.

The Olympic Stadium built for the 2008 Beijing Olympics in China. It was nicknamed the 'Bird's Nest' because of its shape.

Olympic facts and stats

2000 At the Sydney Games, the Bahamas won the women's 4 x 100-metres relay, the smallest nation ever to win a team gold.

2004 In the Athens Games, a man with an advert written on his chest gatecrashed a diving event and jumped from the diving board in a tutu, shouting: "I love you".

2004 Eighteen-year old US swimmer Michael Phelps won six gold medals and two bronze medals at the Athens Games.

2008 Michael Phelps won another eight gold medals at the Beijing Olympics to become the most successful Summer Games Olympian ever.

The 2012 Summer Olympics and the Paralympics are set to take place in London, UK. The Summer Games will feature 26 sports held in venues around London and the rest of the country.

At the Closing Ceremony of the Beijing Games, in 2008, the Olympic flag was passed from the Mayor of Beijing to the Mayor of London. Building had already begun to turn part of London into a giant Olympic Park for the Games. The main stadium is designed to hold 80,000 people and is positioned on an island surrounded by water, with bridges leading up to it.

Olympic venues

Modern Summer Olympic Games have one main stadium, a swimming pool complex and a selection of other venues where special events such as sailing and rowing take place. In the UK, sailing is going to be held off the coast of Weymouth in Dorset. Football will take place in stadiums around the country, including Wales and Scotland, and tennis will be held on the world-famous courts at Wimbledon.

Women's boxing will be a new sport at the London Olympics in 2012. This hopeful boxer stands in front of the London logo.

Amazing Olympics

Four thousand trees are to be planted in the London Olympic Park for a green and leafy effect.

The green Games

Organisers of the London Olympics are aiming to make it the greenest Games yet. The Olympic Park will have gardens to visit, wildlife areas and thousands of specially-planted trees. The organisers will use as much environmentally-friendly technology as they can, and expect the stadium and the Olympic Village to be re-used after the Games for homes and events. The cost of the Olympics runs into many billions, but supporters say that its facilities will benefit the country in the long run.

The design for the 115-metre-high spiral sculpture, the Orbit Tower, at the London Games.

Olympic facts and stats

2012 The Olympic torch will travel around the UK before it reaches London. Up to 8,000 people will take part in the torch-carrying relay.

2012 It's thought that up to one in three people worldwide may watch the London Olympic Opening Ceremony on TV.

2012 Women's boxing will be a new Olympic sport in 2012.

2012 There will be a record 5,000 drug tests on athletes at the London Games.

OLYMPIC FUTURE

Olympic Games are planned years into the future. They need lots of organising, from designing and building the venues to looking after visitors, making deals with sponsors and choosing designs such as the official logo and poster.

The 2014 Winter Olympics are due to be held in Sochi in Russia, and the 2016 Summer Olympics and Paralympics are going to take place in Rio de Janeiro, Brazil. These cities are already busy with their preparations and the IOC will be checking on their progress. Meanwhile other countries around the world are planning bids to host future Olympics, deciding on the best city to put forward as a location and creating virtual 3D pictures of how their Games might look.

Olympic designs

Once a city has been selected, it's time to start organising the marketing – choosing designs for logos, posters and even designs for the medals and the outfits that judges and referees wear. One of the designs redone for each Games is a set of pictograms, symbols for each sport, that are used on signs and posters at Olympic venues.

⬤ The 2010 Winter Olympics were held at Vancouver in Canada. The 2014 Winter Olympics will be held at Sochi in Russia.

▶ A London Olympics pictogram. Every sport has one.

The Youth Olympics

The newest Olympic event is the Youth Olympics, to be held every four years just like the main Games. Young athletes between the ages of 14 and 18 take part, to experience world class competition and perhaps go on to appear in the main Olympics in the future. The first Summer Youth Games was staged in Singapore in 2010 and the first Winter Youth Olympics takes place in Innsbruck, Austria, in 2012. The 2014 Summer Youth Olympics will be held in Nanjing in China.

△ A virtual picture of how the Olympic Park will look at Rio de Janeiro, Brazil, in 2016.

Amazing Olympics

At the Youth Olympics the judges and officials at the Games are young people, as well as the athletes.

Olympic facts and stats

Rio De Janeiro in Brazil will be the first South American city ever to host an Olympic Games.

No Olympic Games have ever been held in Africa.

India has never hosted the Games, despite having one of the largest populations of any country.

The 2012 Olympics has two official mascots, Wenlock and Mandeville, characters shaped like drops of steel from the Olympic stadium.

GLOSSARY

Amateur athlete Someone who doesn't earn money from their sport, which is not their full-time job.

Apartheid The segregation (separation) of black and white people in South Africa during part of the 20th century, that led to South Africa being banned from the Olympics.

Archery Shooting at targets using a bow and arrows.

Boycott Refusing to take part in something as a protest.

Broadcasting rights Permission to show the Olympics on TV. Broadcasting companies pay the Olympic organisers for this.

City states Cities in ancient Greece that governed themselves, with their own laws and customs.

Cold War A period between the 1950s and 1980s when there was suspicion and hostility between the Communist countries of the Soviet Union and Western democratic countries of North America and Europe.

Communism A way of organising a country so that everything is owned by the state and all the profits are shared between the people.

Equestrian An event involving horses.

Feng shui A Chinese belief that objects should be positioned in a certain way, to bring harmony.

IOC International Olympic Committee, the organisation that runs the Olympic Games. It is headed by the President of the IOC.

Licensing Selling the rights to companies to put Olympic logos and mottos on their products.

Logo Official badge. Each Olympic Games chooses its own logo.

Marathon A long-distance running race.

Mascot A cartoon character chosen to symbolise an Olympic Games.

Nazi A member of the National Socialist German Workers' Party, which came to power in Germany in 1933 under the leadership of Adolf Hitler.

Olympia The site of the first Olympics, held in ancient Greece in 776 BCE.

Olympiad An Olympic event held every four years.

Olympic motto *Citius, Altius, Fortius* – Latin for 'Higher, Faster, Stronger.'

Olympic oath A promise made by athletes and judges to abide by the rules and honour the values and spirit of the Olympic Games.

Olympic rings The logo of the Olympic Games, made up of five rings representing Africa, Asia, America, Europe and Oceania, on a white background symbolising peace.

Olympic torch A flame brought from Olympia in Greece to the Olympic stadium in the host city.

Olympic Village Accommodation built for the athletes taking part in the Games.

Pagan The follower of a religion that worships nature.

Pankration A mixture of boxing and wrestling that was an event in the ancient Greek Olympics.

Performance-enhancing drugs Drugs taken to make an athlete perform better (also called 'doping').

Pictogram A simple picture used as a symbol.

Professional athlete Someone whose sport is their full-time job, from which they earn money.

Quarantine A period of isolation for a person, animal or plant, in order to prevent the spread of infection.

Rowing cox The person who steers the boat and helps keep the crew in time with each other.

Sponsor A company that pays to get its products used and displayed at the Olympic Games or elsewhere.

Sprinter A fast runner.

Track and field event An event that takes place on the athletic running track or in the centre of the running track (eg long jump or javelin-throwing).

World Anti-Doping Agency Set up by the International Olympic Committee to test athletes for illegal drug-taking. WADA for short.

Youth Olympics Summer and Winter Olympic Games held every four years for athletes aged between 14 and 18.

Zeus King of the ancient Greek gods, honoured at the ancient Olympic Games.

Modern Summer Olympic Games Timeline

1896 Athens, Greece

1900 Paris, France

1904 St. Louis, USA

1908 London, Great Britain

1912 Stockholm, Sweden

1916 Cancelled due to First World War

1920 Antwerp, Belgium

1924 Paris, France

1928 Amsterdam, Netherlands

1932 Los Angeles, USA

1936 Berlin, Germany

1940 Cancelled due to Second World War

1944 Cancelled due to Second World War

1948 London, Great Britain

1952 Helsinki, Finland

1956 Melbourne, Australia

1960 Rome, Italy (First Paralympic Summer Games also held)

1964 Tokyo, Japan

1968 Mexico City, Mexico

1972 Munich, West Germany

1976 Montreal, Canada

1980 Moscow, USSR

1984 Los Angeles, USA

1988 Seoul, South Korea

1992 Barcelona, Spain

1996 Atlanta, USA

2000 Sydney, Australia

2004 Athens, Greece

2008 Beijing, China

2012 London, Great Britain

2016 Rio de Janeiro, Brazil

Winter Olympics Timeline

1924 Chamonix, France

1928 St. Moritz, Switzerland

1932 Lake Placid, USA

1936 Garmisch, Germany

1940 Cancelled due to Second World War

1944 Cancelled due to Second World War

1948 St. Moritz, Switzerland

1952 Oslo, Norway

1956 Cortina d'Ampezzo, Italy

1960 Squaw Valley, USA

1964 Innsbruck, Austria

1968 Grenoble, France

1972 Sapporo, Japan

1976 Innsbruck, Austria

1976 First Paralympic Winter Games held Ornskoldsvik, Sweden

1980 Lake Placid, USA

1984 Sarajevo, Yugoslavia (now Bosnia)

1988 Calgary, Canada

1992 Albertville, France

1994 Lillehammer, Norway

1998 Nagano, Japan

2002 Salt Lake City, USA

2006 Turin, Italy

2010 Vancouver, Canada

2014 Sochi, Russia

Useful Olympic websites

www. olympic.org The official website of the Olympic Movement.

www.olympic.org.uk Official site for the British Olympic teams.

www. london2012.com The official website of the London Summer Olympics, 2012.

www.paralympics.org The official website of the Paralympics.

www.bbc.co.uk/history/greeks/greek_olympics Find out about the history of the ancient Greek Games.

INDEX

Here are the lists of contents for each title in *The Olympics*...

History
The birth of the Olympics • Olympics reborn • Faster, higher, stronger
Hard times and heroes • Cold War Olympics • Sporting Sixties
Triumphs and disaster • TV Times • New teams, new hope
Hi-tech, high cost • The 2012 Olympics • Olympic future

Scandals
All about the Olympics • Ancient trouble • New games, new problems
Money vs love • Politics wins • Protests and tragedy • Bribes for votes
Doping to win • Caught! • Cheating one-offs
Medical matters • Future shocks

Events
All about the Olympics • Track events • Field events • Aquatic events
Equestrian events • Cycling events • Target shooting
Combat sports • Summer team sports • Racket sports • Boat sports
Strength and technique • Winter Olympics

Records
All about Olympic records • Fastest men
Fastest women • Highest and longest • Super-strongest
Endurance records • In it together – team sports
Water golds • Bullseye champions • Scoring high
Paralympic record-breakers • In the snow